INTRODUCTION TO THE JEWISH SOURCES

Preserving History, Structure, and Heart

A **BE KY** Book ©

S. Creeger, BAJS, MTh.

This booklet is a BEKY Book publication:
Books Encouraging the Kingdom of Yeshua.
www.bekybooks.com

ISBN-13: 9780996183925

DEDICATION

Thanks be to Adonai, who has preserved my life and made all things possible. You have blessed me with the gift of my husband Boaz, who has sheltered me with his love, continually encouraged me, and worked tirelessly so that I may study. I love you both.

CONTENTS

GLOSSARY

Amidah - also known as the *Shmoneh Esrei* prayer (eighteen benedictions) is the central prayer in the synagogue service.

Amoraim – explainers, interpreters, expounders. Typically the rabbis cited in the Gemara who lived both in Palestine and Babylonia from approximately 220 CE-500 CE.

Gemara – the rabbis' commentary on the Mishnah.

Halakha – literally "the way to walk", they are religious rulings on how to perform the commandments.

Midrash – intensive deductive type of study the rabbis employ, credited to Ezra for development.

Mishnah – the codified Oral Law compiled by Judah HaNasi, composed of six orders (sederim) and sixty-three tractates.

Mitzvot –the commandments found in the Bible.

Sanhedrin – the ruling body of rabbis divided into two sects known as the Pharisees and the Sadducees.

Shema – "Hear, O Israel, the Lord, our God, the Lord is One" considered the confession of Jewish faith.

Talmud – the Oral Law includes the Mishnah and Gemara.

Tanakh – The Old Testament an acronym for Torah, Neviim, and Ketuvim; respectively, the first five books of the Bible, Prophets, Writings i.e. Psalms and Chronicles.

Tannaim – from the Aramaic "tena" to teach; the rabbis mentioned in the Mishnah who lived in Palestine between 10 CE-220 CE. They were teachers of the Oral Law.

Tefillin – Phylacteries worn on the head and arm during prayer.

Tosafot - a collection of commentaries from Rashi's male relatives and others. The views presented may agree with Rashi but sometimes the opinions expressed are different.

Zugot – literally "pairs". There were five pairs of rabbis who had dual authority in succession following Antigonus of Socho (the last of the Great Assembly). Their rule ended with Hillel and Shammai.

PREFACE

There is a great gap outside of Orthodox Judaism in regard to exposure, understanding, and even relevancy in the study and application of ancient Jewish texts. In the modern world, it can be difficult for a person to perceive the value of Oral Torah study. "We have the written Torah, that's enough, right? Anything else is man's own idea and application" is a common objection. Another objection is "The Oral Torah was compiled almost two thousand years ago. What can those rabbis have to say to me that would be relevant for my life today?"

For those from a background in Protestantism, the concept of a central body of leaders having authority is a foreign one. For someone from a Catholic background, it is easier to grasp a continual historical transmission of recorded decisions. For Protestants and Catholics, it may be difficult to see the rationale in studying texts that record the debates and subsequent differences in decisions between these same leaders, let alone feel comfortable with the idea that both parties have elucidated the Word of God; therefore, either decision can be acceptable for application.

Alas, Judaism is not Christianity and neither is Messianic Judaism.

For many, the purpose of Oral Torah study is to establish *Halakhah* (religious laws) and provide guidance on how to fulfill the *Mitzvot* (commandments) found in the written Torah, but it is so much more than that. Thorough Torah study, both Oral and Written, will provide a comprehensive worldview of how the Torah permeates every facet of life. One gains so much more insight than just "how" or "the correct way" to do something. It equips an individual to see all things with a Torah perspective so that each subject can be understood, related to, and ultimately acted upon in a righteous manner.

This book's purpose is to:

- Awaken a renewed interest in Oral Torah study for those who are familiar with it
- Kindle a desire to learn for those who have never studied Oral Torah
- Foster honor and respect for the rabbis and Torah scholars who went before us
- Better understand the difficult decisions facing the rabbis who had to maintain continuity in tradition and education as their religious world collapsed following the Second Temple destruction and subsequent exile

To meet these objectives, we will examine the development and codification of the Oral Torah and some historical events that precipitated the written document, Talmud, which was previously only orally-transmitted information. The fact that we have in our possession today this remarkable and unique document testifies to the rabbis' determination for Israel not to lose their connection to their past. This connection is maintained against almost insurmountable odds from foreign pressures.

May we humbly open its pages and draw nearer to HaShem (God).

INTRODUCTION

Judaism has a long historical interpretive tradition. That chain of historical transmission starts with Moses at Mt. Sinai.

> Moses received the Torah from Sinai and transmitted it to Joshua, and Joshua to the Elders, and the Elders to the Prophets, and the Prophets to the Men of the Great Assembly. (Pirke Avot 1.1)

According to Jewish tradition, Ezra founded the Great Assembly. The Men of the Great Assembly consisted of 120 sages (not all lived during the same time). Among these were Zechariah, Seraiah (Ezra's father), Haggai, Reelaiah, Nehemiah, Mordecai (from the book of Esther), Ezra, Daniel, Chananyah, Mishael, and Azariah (Daniel's companions in the fire). Ezra was the chief judge, so these men were often referred to as Ezra's Court or Ezra's group.

> They composed blessings and prayers, sanctifications and *havdalahs*.
> (Berachot 33a).

Havdalahs were the different divisions found within the *havdalah* blessings. *Havdalah* means to make a separation or distinction; it is the word used by the rabbis for blessings and prayers that are recited to bring attention to and make the distinction between times of varying degrees of holiness: Shabbat from the work week, the festival days from work days, and Shabbat from the Festival days.

To help the people mark the difference, the rabbis decreed that there needed to be a formal separation of the holy and mundane. This is accomplished by pronouncing a havdalah. For instance, after Shabbat ends, Jews light a candle of six wicks, pour a cup of wine, and have a container of spices. The family says blessings, drinks the wine, smells the spices, and closes out the Shabbat, ushering in the new workweek. Under the leadership of Esther and Mordecai, the festival of Purim was also instituted at this time.

Pirke Avot

These three maxims would be used as guide for teachers and expounders of the Torah:

> They said three things: Be deliberate in judgment, raise up many disciples, and make a fence around the Torah. (Pirke Avot 1.1)

"Be deliberate in judgment" is from Proverbs 25:2: "It is the glory of God to conceal a matter, but the glory of kings is to search out a matter." The word for *search*, תָקַר, means to examine, ascertain, and investigate. Although the original intent was a caution to actual judges so they would not conclude a case hastily, but examine it thoroughly prior to rendering judgment, it came to be understood in Rabbinic Judaism as argument or debate. This deliberation is what is happening in the Talmud when the rabbis study the questions posed to them from every angle and point of view, even taking into account every possible, if somewhat improbable, outcome or event; every answer must be derived from the Torah.

"Raise up many disciples." The goal in Judaism is not just to impart knowledge of the Torah. A great purpose of the Torah is to remove segmented thinking and provide a comprehensive worldview so that one can embrace how the Torah relates to everything in the world, physical and spiritual; this worldview also acknowledges how those things relate to one another. The ability to not just have an intellectual knowing of this, but to fully incorporate it in one's life will revolutionize one's response to everything. In their role as Torah teachers, rabbis were cautioned not to make followers of themselves, but to develop lovers of HaShem [1] and of His Word.

"Make a fence around the Torah" has often been a misunderstood statement. The rabbis never intended for it to be a set of rigid and complex decrees placed upon the people. It was always understood to mean the precautions that would be taken to guard the holy revelation, to protect against its violation so that the truth would always be available for one to access. In many ways, the fence or hedge made the difference between life and death since some violations are punishable by death.

Something similar is found in Genesis 3:22-24. HaShem set Adam and Chavah out of the Garden of Eden following their consumption of the fruit from the tree of the knowledge of good and evil. He lovingly set them out for their own good so that they would not eat from the tree of life and live forever in their current state. Prior to their breaking the commandment of eating from that particular tree, things were clearly good or evil. The disobedience brought confusion, and the "knowing" of good and evil would always be "mixed" and much more difficult to discern. HaShem set the Cherubim with flaming swords to **guard the way** to the tree of life. The swords made sure the way could always be found. It was not punishment, but life-saving action. The hedge around the Torah provides the same thing: it guards the way so the Torah is preserved.

The Need for Clarification

The written Torah contains 613 total commandments. Three hundred and sixty-five are negative commandments equaling the number of days in a solar year, so one is warned each day of the year not to transgress them. Two hundred and forty-eight are positive, which represent organs and limbs (bones that have sinew and flesh around them), reminding

1. HaShem literally means The Name and refers to the most sacred name for God, usually translated as LORD.

13

one that the whole body should be in submission to HaShem to perform his commandments. Ideally, the main motivation to keep the *mitzvot* should be love of HaShem.

> "...Greater is he who performs (the commandments) from love than he who performs them from fear" (Sotah 31a).

Judaism, like Christianity and Islam, is a text-based religion, meaning it draws inspiration and ethical rules of conduct from written documents. Jews believe the texts to have been given by God for instruction. The most desirable result of studying these texts is submission and application to the words written, developing a desire to draw near and please God out of love, not fear. The most beautiful response from study of Torah and the obedience that follows should cause one to say with wonder "For my sake was the world made."

Many of the commandments in the Written Torah are indecipherable without the clarification found in the Oral Torah. An example of this is Deuteronomy 6:8:

> And you shall bind them as a sign on your hand and they shall be טטפות frontals (*tefillin*/ phylacteries) on your forehead.

The word for frontals or phylacteries has no actual translation value [2]. It is found three times in the Torah, and each time it represents this item that is placed between the eyes. What is the "them" that one is to bind, the "they" that are like frontals on the forehead?

The Talmud gives the answer, rules for the exact standards and materials to make the tefillin boxes and straps. The Talmud describes what color they must be, black, blessings to say, and how to wrap the leather bindings. The Talmud specifies the scripture passages written on parchment within them will be Deuteronomy 6:4-9 and 11:13-21, Exodus 13:1-10 and 13:11-16.

2. Strong's 2903 from an unused root meaning go around, or bind.

14

The wearing of them is to connect the head, heart, and hands to work as a cohesive holy unit for HaShem. They are sacred ritual objects, and as such may not be worn in defiled places or bathrooms. The wearer must avoid all forms of evil both in thought and in deed and keep his mind and body pure while wearing them. They are worn in the mornings only and not on Shabbat or Festival days. Do not eat a regular meal while wearing them or sleep in them. When they become worn out and can no longer be used, they are put away in a respectful manner, not thrown out in the trash. The Oral Law supplies specific information to help perform the mitzvot.

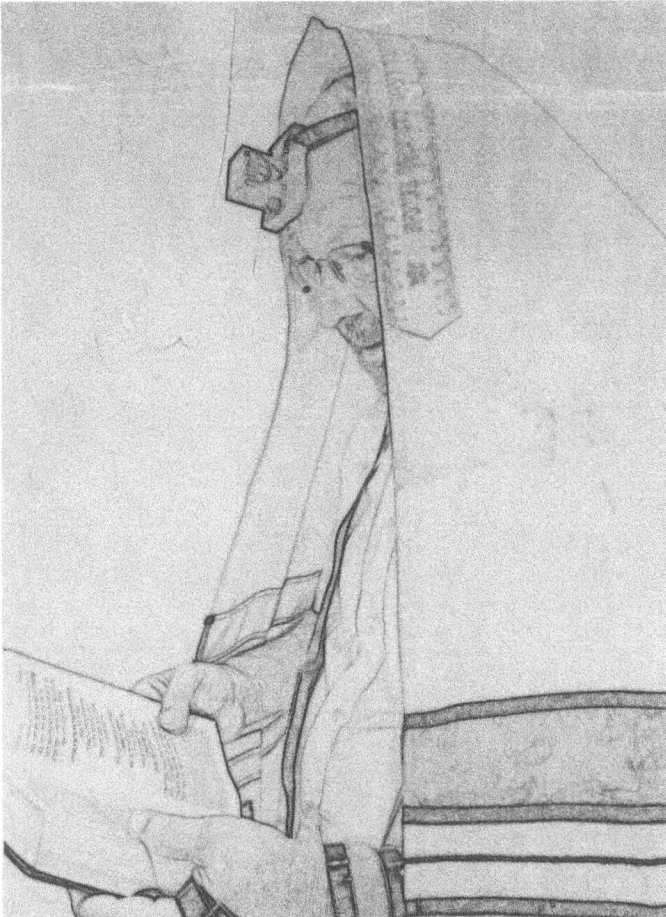

A Messianic singer recounted an experience that is illustrative of how individual interpretations can be sincere, yet strange. She ministered in a congregation where she saw a man wearing a Post It Note covered with Bible verses on his forehead. When she inquired, she was told it was that man's interpretation of what phylacteries were; it was how he was keeping the commandment. That sounds a little strange, but this is a sample of the anomalies that may occur with disregard for the Oral Torah that elucidates how to perform this commandment and others.

QUESTIONS FOR REVIEW AND APPLICATION

1. What advantage is there in having a historical chain of oral transmission of laws?

2. Define *havdalah*. How would the observance of *havdalah* benefit you?

3. Identify and expound upon the Three Maxims the Men of the Great Assembly developed.

4. Even if you are not a Torah teacher, how might, "Be deliberate in judgment" be applied in your own life?

5. Name some specifics found in the Talmud that clarify how to observe the mitzvot found in Deuteronomy 6:8.

1

FOUNDATION FOR THE ORAL LAW

The Written Torah hints at a parallel text of law in Deuteronomy 12:21:

> ...and you may slaughter of your herd
> and flock...as I have commanded
> you.

Although Israel is commanded to sacrifice from this verse, nowhere in the Written Torah are found the instructions on how to exactly fulfill this. The Oral Law/Talmud, however, does contain many explicit instructions on *shechitah* (ritual slaughter), the most humane way to slaughter kosher animals.

In Judaism, Biblical decrees always have more authority than rabbinical decrees. For that reason, it's hard for many to understand why such honor would be given to the Oral Torah. One answer is found in Deuteronomy 17:8-13:

> If any case is too difficult for you
> to decide, between one kind of
> homicide or another, between
> one kind of lawsuit or another, and
> between one kind of assault or
> another, being cases of dispute in your

courts, then you shall arise and go up to the place which the Lord your God chooses.

So you shall come to the Levitical priest or the judge, who is *in office* in those days, and you shall inquire *of them*, and they will declare to you the verdict in the case.

And you shall do according to the terms of the verdict which they declare to you from that place which the Lord chooses; and you shall be careful to observe according to all that they teach you.

According to the terms of the law which they teach you, and according to the verdict which they tell you, you shall do; you shall not turn aside from the word which they declare to you, to the right or the left. And the man who acts presumptuously by not listening to the priest who stands there to serve the Lord your God, nor to the judge, that man shall die; thus you shall purge the evil from Israel. Then all the people will hear and be afraid, and will not act presumptuously again.

It is apparent that HaShem gave the offices of Priest and Judge the authority to interpret the Torah and pass verdicts (laws, actions) for those who are inquiring. The purpose was to keep the covenant people from acting יְזִדוּן (yezeh-doon) presumptuously. The root זדון means evil, wickedness, malice, insolent, wanton, as well as presumptuous. When an individual acts presumptuously, he fails to observe the limits of what is permitted or appropriate. This can lead to behavior that is brazen, arrogant, and familiar.

There has been no active judge or priest since the Second Temple destruction. The responsibility to mediate disputes, resolve conflicts, and answer inquiries of a religious or Halakhic nature are now solely the duties of the rabbis. In the *Brit Hadasha* [3] is the same instruction in Hebrews 13:17:

> Obey your leaders, and submit *to them*;
> for they keep watch over your souls,
> as those who will give an account. Let
> them do this with joy and not with grief,
> for this would be unprofitable for you.

This does not imply that one should blindly follow leaders, but rather that one should hold them in honor and respect for the number of years studying and learning that they have accomplished and the enormously difficult task assigned to them to care for us. Even Moshe, the greatest leader in the Tanakh [4], became frustrated with the people of Israel. Individuals can be challenging to those in authority at one time or another.

Unlike other instructions in Scripture, this reminder in Hebrews 13 is found only in the book written to the Messianic Jews, perhaps because this was a continuation of a traditional Jewish practice of rabbinic authority. This is another example of the beauty of the continuity in Scripture.

Rabbinic Authority

In speaking of rabbinic authority, many shudder at the terminology, yet all have been one of the parties in some type of authority relationship, i.e, a parent to child, teacher to student, employer to employee, and even as citizens in our respective countries. In each of these relationships, one is in a position of authority, and the other has surrendered autonomy to the one in authority. Religious authority is a natural extension of those relationships.

One day when my son was four years old, he was musing

3. The New Testament

4. Old Testament

to himself audibly and said, "I can't wait to grow up so I can do whatever I want." I was driving at the time and had just stopped the car at the red light. I asked him did he think I was able to do whatever I wanted; after all, I had just obeyed a traffic signal. He guessed not. It was a great time to impress on him that rules are not only for ourselves, but for those around us. It is important to remind ourselves that we keep Torah not just for ourselves, but for others as well.

To begin to understand the enormous responsibility and sacred trust that was placed upon the rabbis and Torah scholars in Judea and Babylon, let's examine some historical events.

QUESTIONS FOR REVIEW AND APPLICATION

1. What is the Hebrew word for the ritual slaughter of kosher animals?

Where are those instructions found?

2. What is the Hebrew word translated as presumptuously in Deuteronomy 17:12, 13?

3. What does the root זדון mean?

4. Review the verses Deuteronomy 17:8-13. Is it possible for an individual to act זדון out of ignorance? Why or why not?

5. What is the Biblical injunction for prevention of זדון ?

6. Review verses Hebrews 13:17 and Deuteronomy 17:11. What is the purpose of this authority? Who benefits from the authority?

Historical Development

Israel became a divided kingdom shortly after King Solomon's death in 930 BCE. His son Rehoboam, upon ascending to the kingship, was unsympathetic to the requests of the people to lighten the yoke of taxation that had been set upon them by his father, King Solomon. Ignoring the counsel of the elders, he instead embraced the counsel of his friends. He responded to the people, "Whereas my father loaded you with a heavy yoke; I will add to your yoke; my father disciplined you with whips, but I will discipline you with scorpions." (I Kings 12:11)

Needless to say, this was not well received, and the ten Northern tribes split and established themselves as a separate nation, calling themselves Israel under the kingship of Jeroboam ben Nebat. Jeroboam had been a rebellious leader in Solomon's labor force and was a fugitive hiding in Egypt until Solomon died.

The two remaining tribes of Judah and Benjamin (and some from Levi) remained under the leadership of Solomon's son Rehoboam, and they were called Judea, which is where the word Jew is derived from. The reason there are some people from the tribe of Levi is that the tribe of Levi lived throughout the land of Israel since they did not have land specifically appointed for them. The kingdom would never again be whole, and the Northern and Southern kingdoms throughout their existence would each have many kings.

Fast forward to 727 BCE. Biblical accounts found in 2 Kings 17:1-6 and other documents document that Hoshea was king over Israel in Samaria. He was a loyal vassal of Tiglath-pileser, King of Assyria. Following Tiglath-pileser's death in 727 BCE, Shalmaneser V ascended to the throne. Hoshea had a political strategy of appeasement and defiance toward Shalmaneser V. During his period of defiance, Hoshea became involved in a revolt that started in the western part of the Assyrian Empire. During that time, he communicated with So, the King of Egypt, presumably looking for help or possibly to form an anti-Assyrian alliance. He also withheld the annual tribute to Shalmaneser V. Unfortunately, Egypt did not respond to his request, and Hoshea was imprisoned as a result of his actions.

While Hoshea was in custody, Shalmaneser V invaded the whole of Israel, marched to Samaria (the capital), and laid siege to the city (2 Kings 17:5). The siege lasted three years, and the city fell in 722 BCE. Shalmaneser V died a few months afterward, and Sargon II seized his throne. Samaria was now under Assyrian control, but Sargon II had no time to address what to do with Samaria or its inhabitants, for he immediately had to fight two major revolts in his empire which erupted when he became king. It would be 720 BCE before Sargon II would get back to the issue of what to do about Samaria. His decision was to incorporate Samaria as part of the Assyrian empire and continue the deportation of the Israelites.

Although it had been a practice of Assyrian kings to deport captives, it was Tiglath-pileser who employed the practice of two-way relocations. In 2 Kings 17:6, the king of Assyria transported Israelites to Assyria, and in 2 Kings 17:24, he repopulated the cities of Samaria with people from Babylon and other areas. The Northern Kingdom was no more, and the people were assimilated into the Assyrian populace. The significance of this is that Israel, or the Jewish people, are found in Judea, the Southern kingdom consisting of the tribes of Benjamin, Judah, and part of Levi.

In 591-592 BCE, Zedekiah, King of Judea (a vassal of Babylon), revolted against Nebuchadnezzar, King of Babylon (2 Kings 24:20). Nebuchadnezzar did not respond immediately to the uprising; he did dispatch an army, and they reached Jerusalem early 587 BCE. They laid siege to Jerusalem for 18 months. For a brief time the city's inhabitants enjoyed a respite when Egyptian aid arrived (Jeremiah 37:5,11), but the Egyptian reinforcements were not enough, and the walls of Jerusalem were breached in the summer of 586 BCE.

Zedekiah was captured in the plains of Jericho while trying to escape at nighttime and was taken before Nebuchadnezzar. Zedekiah's sons were captured and executed before his eyes. Zedekiah was then blinded, bound with bronze fetters, and carried away to Babylon (2 Kings 25:1-7).

The following month, the Babylonian leader commanded that the city of Jerusalem and the Temple be razed. Most of the city's inhabitants were exiled, leaving some of the poorest of the land to be vinedressers and plowmen (2 Kings 25:8-12). According to Jeremiah 52:29, an additional 832 people from Jerusalem also were exiled. Unlike the Assyrians, the Babylonians did not repopulate conquered cities with captive foreigners. Nebuchadnezzar did not rebuild the city or make it a capital city as other conquered cities had been, possibly because Jerusalem had a long history as a hotbed of rebellion.

Nebuchadnezzar set up a military unit of pro-Babylonian Jews and appointed Gedaliah ben Ahikam as governor over the land (II Kings 25:23). They were stationed in Mizpah, about 13 km from Jerusalem. The prophet Jeremiah, once he was released from chains, returned also to Gedaliah at Mizpah and became part of the leadership there (Jeremiah 40:1-9). Both he and Gedaliah urged the people not to resist the Babylonians, but to serve them so that it would go well with them.

Gedaliah's leadership offered a semblance of peace and security, and the remaining Jews who had fled or been exiled to other lands came back to the land of Judah and began to settle around Mizpah, planting crops and harvesting grapes (Jeremiah 40:12). In Jewish tradition, the story is told of how Ishmael ben Nethaniah, along with ten men, came to Mizpah and asked to celebrate Rosh HaShanah with Gedaliah and his men there. Gedaliah had been warned that Ishmael was planning to kill him, but he rebuked the messenger, decrying it as slander (Jeremiah 40:13-16). Gedaliah was indeed killed and many Jews with him, as well as the Babylonian military officers assigned to Gedaliah. The account can be read in Jeremiah 41 and 2 Kings 25:25-26.

In retaliation for Gedaliah's assassination, Nebuchadnezzar deported even more Jews to Babylon. The surviving members of Gedaliah's contingent failed to heed the word of the Lord from Jeremiah and fled to Egypt (Jeremiah 42-43). This ended any autonomy that Judea might have enjoyed following the Babylonian conquest. Jews remember this yearly with a fast following the second day of Rosh HaShanah. This is the fast of the seventh month found in Zechariah 8:19.

QUESTIONS FOR REVIEW AND APPLICATION

1. What caused the nation of Israel to split into two kingdoms?

2. Historically, what happened to the people of the Northern Kingdom?

3. Who first employed the practice of two-way relocation?

What was the significance of the Assyrian deportment of Jewish captives?

4. What Israelite King rebelled against Nebuchadnezzar, King of Babylon?

What was the outcome of his rebellion, personally and nationally?

5. Who was Gedaliah ben Ahikam?

What was he appointed to do?

What happened to him?

6. What was King Nebuchadnezzar's response to the assassination of Gedaliah?

7. What did this mean for the people and the land of Judea?

8. Read Zechariah 8:19. What does the fast of the seventh month commemorate?

What Do We Do Now?

Can you see how serious the national and theological crisis? All ten northern tribes of Israel have been gone for 150 years. The Temple is destroyed, and many Jewish people are dead or exiled. The remaining Jewish community exiled in Babylon wonder if they will disappear and never be heard from again, assimilated into Babylonian culture. How can they prevent what happened to the Northern Kingdom from happening to them? Without a Temple, how can they worship, practice their religion, or maintain their distinctiveness in a foreign land surrounded by gentile influence?

The Biblical account does not provide specific details about the exile, but Ezekiel 8:1, 14:1, and 20:1 document that the elders of Judah gathered at Ezekiel's home. The questions had to have been uppermost in their minds. The only solution that assured the continual distinctiveness of being Jewish was the instruction and application of the Torah.

The Solution: Every question must start and end with Torah, both Oral and Written.

It can be presumed that the exiles had in their possession the laws from Moses, both oral and written, the Psalms, and some of the prophetic writings. It would be under the direction of Ezekiel and the teachings of Ezra that the Jews were reminded of their sacred calling to be a set-apart people. Many scholars believe it was in exile where the synagogue was first developed. This House of Assembly (*Beit HaKnesset*) would be a place for the Scriptures to be read and expounded upon, Hebrew to be taught, prayers offered, and finally it would become a house of worship.

Ezra was the leading teacher (Ezra 7:6); a scribe skilled in the Torah of Moses, he set his heart to study and keep Torah and teach it to the people (Ezra 7:10). The word used for study in 7:10 is *darash,* דרש which means inquire, demand, seek, expound interpret, and explain. It is where the word *darshan* דרשן (preacher) is derived. Ezra used his intense study of Torah to bring very clear understanding to his students. The process of this type of intensive deductive study is called *Midrash*. The rabbis use this interpretive process throughout the rabbinical literature.

Through Ezra and others' instruction, the Jewish people would once again learn Torah and how to be a distinct people, not just in word, but in daily living. His influence would reenergize a dying community and later carry them back to Israel.

In 539 BCE, Cyrus the Great, the ruler of Persia, conquered Babylon, and the Persians then succeeded the Babylonians as the major power player in the Near East. Unlike the Assyrians and the Babylonians, the Persians encouraged the displaced and exiled peoples to return to their respective ancestral lands and reestablish their religious and political institutions so they could serve a supportive role to the new Persian Empire. Under Kings Cyrus and Darius, many of the Jews would return to their homeland and rebuild the Temple, continuing the tradition handed down to them by the Men of the Great Assembly.

The Great Assembly

The Men of the Great Assembly were not only entrusted with the sacred transmission of Torah, but a type of study (*Midrash*) to which Torah teachers of many later generations would conform.

It is not known exactly when the Great Assembly, or as some manuscripts call it, the Great Synagogue, ceased to exist, but the institution that followed it was known as the Sanhedrin. In Hebrew it was called the *Beit Din HaGadol* (The Great Court House). The Sanhedrin differed from the Great Assembly because it was not structured to be an academic institution for Torah study. Its main purpose was to oversee the cultural and spiritual life of Jews. Theoretically, for any communal problems that would arise in synagogues or courts that could not be decided, the Sanhedrin's decision was the final authority. Historically, every decision that they made was recorded and became part of the Oral Law.

There are varying opinions over how many members made up the Sanhedrin, from 70 to 71. Over time the differences between the members would result in two separate sects known as the Sadducees and the Pharisees. It's thought that there were two chambers, one political, and the other judicial. The political chamber was ruled by the Sadducees, and their head was the High Priest. The Pharisee chamber oversaw cultural and religious observance, and it was headed up equally by two leaders known as the zugot (pairs). In Second Temple times, the Sadducees and Pharisees struggled with each other to control the Sanhedrin.

Zugot

In Tractate *Avot*, the record of transmission of the Oral and Written Torah continues from the Men of the Great Assembly to Simeon the Just. From Simeon the Just, it was transmitted to one of his students, Antigonius of Socho, and from there to two individuals, Jose ben Joezer of Zeredah and Jose ben Jochanan of Jerusalem. They were the first of five *zugot* (pairs) of rabbis having dual authority in succession, the last and the most prominent being Hillel and Shammai. For each pair, one would be *nasi* (prince, i.e. president) and the other would be *av beit din* (father of the Court of Law i.e. vice president). Hillel was *nasi* and Shammai *av beit din*.

These pairs instituted some type of needed reform, such as the requirement that every Jewish community must establish and maintain a school for children where Torah, prayers, and other subjects would be taught. Another reform was the requirement that the *ketuba* (marriage contract) must include that the wife upon divorce or death of her husband was legally able to demand her portion from his property or his property that has been inherited by others [5]. One pair is most remembered for saying, "Get yourself a teacher," indicating that the best way to learn Torah was in a student-teacher relationship.

Hillel was born in Babylon and migrated to Judea. For about forty years (30 BCE- 10 CE), he was one of the greatest leaders in his community. He was loved for his modesty, tenderness, and great patience. He was respected for his brilliance in Torah. The Talmud records once when the Jewish community in Judea was uncertain (because they had forgotten a law) and asked whether they could slaughter the Pesach offering if Passover eve fell on Saturday, Hillel answered yes and provided the texts to support his answer. The Talmud records him as a scholar who was willing to teach Torah to a heathen who requested instruction. He did it with abundant patience and kindness (Shabbat 31a). He used to say, "If I am not for myself, who is for me? And if I am for myself, what am I? If not now, when?" (Avot 1.14)

Shammai was a contemporary of Hillel from Judea. He was quick-tempered and did not possess the gentleness and patience of Hillel. The Talmud records the same heathen (who went to Hillel) coming to Shammai to learn Torah, but he only wanted to learn the Written Torah. Shammai rebuked him and sent him away (Shabbat 31a). Shammai was zealous for the Torah and was very strict in his adherence and narrow in his view of it. Once his daughter-in-law gave birth during Sukkot, and Shammai tore a hole into the roof of the room where she lay and placed s'chah [6] over it so that his grandson could observe the law of dwelling in a sukkah (Sukkot 28a). As a baby, the grandson was exempt from observing the commandments, but Shammai insisted it was not too early for the parents to train him in Torah. Shammai used to say, "Make the study of Torah a fixed habit; say little and do much; and receive every man with a pleasant face." (Avot 1.15)

Hillel and Shammai each had many students

5. The new regulation placed the husband's property under lien. Prior to this it was an unwritten moral obligation, and the wife and her dependents were at the mercy of the divorced spouse or heirs to provide her portion. This ensured that she would be provided for.

6. Covering for a roof on a sukkah; can be made from bamboo, tree branches, unfinished wood etc...

gather around them. As a result, two separate and contradictory systems of thought in the Torah developed. The school of Shammai was a strict constructionist school. The school of Hillel interpreted laws with a view to making them easier to observe. Both schools stressed the need to keep the Oral Torah, and both were extremely influential in developing *Halakha* (religious law).

QUESTIONS FOR REVIEW AND APPLICATION

1. What concerns did the exiled Jewish community in Babylon have?

Why are those concerns so pressing?

What is the consistent answer to those concerns?

2. What is the Beit HaKnesset?

Where was it developed?

What was its purpose?

3. What is Midrash?

Who can benefit from it?

What is its importance?

4. What institute replaced the Great Assembly?
How did that institute differ from the Great Assembly?

5. Define Zugot.

What were their respective positions?

What are some of the reforms they instituted?

6. Who was Hillel?

7. Who was Shammai?

8. How did the respective schools differ from one another?

Revolt!

Nothing is conceived in a vacuum, so history aids in understanding the position in which the rabbis found themselves.

Israel had been under Roman rule since 63 B.C.E. The people of Israel were subjected to taxes, corrupt tax collectors, and Roman procurators ruling over them who had no knowledge or respect of local customs and traditions. The procurator Florus stole the silver from the Temple treasury. Emperor Caligula declared himself a deity and demanded his statue be placed in the Temple. Another emperor demanded that the appointment of the *Cohen HaGadol* (High Priest) be made by Rome. These individuals selected for High Priest were not from the lineage of Aaron, but were generally pro-Roman Jews.

By 66 C.E. the Jews were very frustrated and a revolt broke out in the north. The zealots who were responsible for rousing the people to fight experienced a victory against a very small Roman militia. This caused them to believe HaShem (God) was on their side and that they would be victorious. After this skirmish, Rome sent in many troops and the casualties for Israel were enormous in Galilee. The zealots marched to Jerusalem, fighting small battles along the way. Shortly after they entered Jerusalem, the Roman army surrounded the city. Rome allowed no one to enter the city, but they did, however, allow the dead to be removed and buried, and anyone who wanted to leave Jerusalem could do so, surrendering as they exited.

The zealots were adamant that no one leave the city, and they began to kill anyone who tried to leave. The rabbis pushed for the people to surrender, knowing they would lose and that many would die before the revolt ended. The zealots, infuriated with the rabbis, began to enter the *yeshivot* (religious schools) and kill the teachers and students. In an effort to force the inhabitants of the city to join the fighting, the zealots burned the store houses containing the provisions needed to endure the siege, causing additional suffering for their own people.

Rabbi Yochanan ben Zakkai (a student of Hillel) had his students place him in a coffin and carry him outside the city. He surrendered himself to Vespasian and prophesied that Vespasian would be made Caesar. In response to the prophecy, Vespasian offered to grant him one request. Yochanan ben Zakkai requested permission to settle in and start a yeshiva in Yavneh with its wise men. He asked for the family of Rabbi Gamliel to be spared and for physicians to treat some other rabbis who were ill (Gittin 56b).

In 70 C.E. the walls of Jerusalem were breached and the Second Temple was destroyed. The Jews were prohibited from living in Jerusalem and the remaining rabbis began to teach in Yavneh. Rabbi Yochanan ben Zakkai had the foresight to see that if nothing changed, there would be no Jewish communal life in Judea because all of the individuals educated in Torah would not be alive to continue to teach and train others.

Teacher to Student

The Oral Law has always been just that, oral. Prior to the destruction of the Second Temple, it was never written down to be made available for public dissemination. In each generation, the leading Torah authority (prophet, or head of the Sanhedrin) would make personal notations about the teachings he had received from his Torah teachers. He would then teach those expanded teachings orally to the people. These personal manuscripts contained the traditionally transmitted laws and the new laws that had been ratified by the Sanhedrin. This was the accepted practice to learn and teach Oral Torah. No one ever taught anything they thought; all teachings were done in the name of the master Torah scholar who had trained them. This was an ancient acknowledgment that plagiarism is a form of theft.

Rabbis felt teacher-to-student was the best way to convey Jewish tradition. Since all of the information was available only orally, no one could pick up a manuscript and say, "No, this is what they meant!" This is why a modern reader simply cannot pick up a copy of the Oral Law text and understand it. It was intended to be taught and learned within the relationship of teacher to student.

No student broke away on his own and started something new. The understanding was that the ones closest to the law who had received the revelation were in the best authoritative position. Hence comes the tradition: Moses to Joshua, Joshua to the elders, the elders to the prophets, the prophets to the Men of the Great Assembly and so on. Learning in such an intimate way from a Torah Scholar, the student could not fail to master the information or the nuances associated with it. The teacher was right there to answer any questions he may have had.

Another local phenomenon in Judea was the Dead Sea Scroll people. They were prolific in their writings and interpretation of texts, but they talked about their study as the "last interpretation of the Law." They saw themselves as people living on the verge of the coming of Messiah. The "last interpretation of the Law" means that nothing comes after it; therefore, they were fairly comfortable in writing down their last interpretation. They treated what they wrote as authoritative.

When something is treated as authoritative, it becomes like a Biblical text. It makes sense that if you have the last and final interpretation of the Bible, there would be no reason not to write it down. "The last" implies you have everything you need and there is nothing more to learn. Hmm...

The rabbis however, are operating under "the correct interpretation of the Law," which is not the same as the final or last interpretation. The rabbis don't want to write down the Oral Law; frankly, they may be afraid of having it written down because **they don't want the interpretation of the text to become as authoritative as the text itself.**

The Oral Law is Recorded

But times have changed. The rabbis knew following the destruction of the Second Temple and the Bar Kokhba rebellion that the level of scholarship was waning [7], Jews were being dispersed far and wide, and the Roman Empire was expanding, which could bode poorly for Jews everywhere. The time had come to write down the Oral Law.

Prior to 200 C.E., there were multiple manuscripts containing rulings on the Oral Law, Scriptural exegesis, personal observations from the rabbis, etc. None of these manuscripts was complete, and many had differing opinions upon the rulings. This led to confusion and chaos, as there was no one authoritative manuscript to provide a standardized learning.

Around 200 C.E., Rabbi Yehudah HaNasi (Judah the Prince), son of Rabbi Shimon ben Gamliel, compiled and redacted the laws from all available manuscripts, often including the different rulings using the rabbis' precise and unique way of wording their decisions. Legal matters, anecdotes, rules of conduct, Scriptural exegesis, and the Temple rituals were placed in a concise and systematic order. This work is called *Mishnah*.

7. Waning because so many Torah scholars and students had been killed, over a million Jews total.
Recording allowed uniformity for teaching Halakhah (religious law) and facilitated study, so the laws could be learned fairly quickly and not be forgotten. Rabbi Yehudah NaNasi's purpose was not to "set the law" and make it unmovable; that would be contrary to the purpose of the rabbis for the Oral Law. Oral Law elucidates difficult texts and shows how to keep the mitzvot, but it is a living thing, fully capable of meeting

the needs of the Jewish community no matter what century in which they lived or what situations would arise about which the Torah did not specifically speak. The Mishnah provided a link between the Jews in Palestine to Jews in the Diaspora. It was received as authoritative (Judah HaNasi's position and respect in the community aided that), and the work endured to bind together the Jewish people despite their geographical distances. It would become the core text of both the Jerusalem and Babylonian Talmudim [8].

8. Plural of Talmud

2

MISHNAH

Although it has just been described in very simple terms, the Mishnah is a very complex work. Historically it portrays Jewish religious and secular life as though Jews still lived in The Land of Israel pre-Temple destruction. It is written very academically, which can make studying it challenging. At times it appears as if the academic discussion is pursued only for its own sake. Debates between the schools of Hillel and Shammai are presented; generally the Pharisean standards are presented as preeminent and the Sadducean rulings as insignificant or heretical if presented at all.

The wording is terse, and no explanations are given for terms used or arguments presented, as it was assumed the reader, both student and teacher, would be familiar with them. The Mishnah is written mostly in Hebrew, but it differs from Biblical Hebrew both in syntax and vocabulary. The language of the Mishnah was not a spoken language, but rather a very formalized language used for learning and to facilitate memorization. There are sections written in Aramaic with words also borrowed from Latin and Greek.

The Mishnah functions as a law (halakhah) book and a textbook. As a law book, it tells what is prohibited and what is permitted; as a textbook it contains a wealth of information and is an authoritative book that all students study. It addresses bluntly and without hesitation matters involving, but not limited to: menstruation, diseased and blemished animals and humans, corpses, genitalia, seminal emissions and discharges, and moldy objects. It explains how vessels of wood, clay, and metal become impure and how to calculate the tithe of produce from trees and crops. It shies away from nothing that an individual could be exposed to, thereby addressing life's concerns.

The word Mishnah משנה is derived from the root *shanah* שנה which means to repeat. This word Mishnah encompasses teaching or learning orally through repetition. Since the Mishnah covers a variety of topics, it is divided into six divisions called "orders" in Hebrew: *Sederim*. These six *Sederim* are in turn divided into tractates *Mashechtot* (literally, texts). There are sixty-three tractates in total. Originally there were sixty tractates; the tractates of *Bava Kamma* (first gate), *Bava Metzia* (middle gate), and *Bava Bathra* (last gate) were at one time a single tractate; while *Makkot* (lashes) was originally combined with *Sanhedrin* (rabbinical court).

There is one tractate that does not deal with any laws; it is called *Pirke Avot* (usually translated as Ethics of the Fathers). It contains sayings from leading Torah scholars throughout the generations. They are spiritually uplifting words rendering moral advice, often with practical application.

Here is an example of what can be found there:

> Rabbi Chanina, who was a deputy of the priests and survived the fall of Jerusalem was quoted as saying: 'Pray for the peace of the government; for, except for the fear of that, we should have swallowed each other alive.'(3.2)
>
> Hillel said: 'Sever not yourself from

the congregation...judge not your associate until you are in his place... say not, "'when I am at leisure I will study-perchance you will never be at leisure.'"(2.5)

Rabbi Ishmael was the grandson of Ishmael ben Elisha, the high priest who was executed at the fall of Jerusalem. He said: 'Be submissive to the ruler, patient under oppression; and receive everyone with cheerfulness.'(3.16)

How are These Connected?

Each seder contains a group of tractates that deal with closely related topics, BUT sometimes a tractate appears in a seder which at first sight seems like it should not belong there.

The First Seder, *Zera'im*, is about agricultural matters. The first tractate found there is *Berachot* (blessings/benedictions). How do blessings or benedictions fit in with agricultural laws? Just like the portions for the priests and Levites first must be separated before the crop is free for common use, Berachot deals with the prayers that a man is obligated to say before he goes about his common day. In regard to food, the same principle applies: a man blesses HaShem, which is man's duty to God (since the Creator supplies the food), before he eats his meal.

In the third Seder *Nashim* (women) are tractates *Nedarim* (vows) and *Nazir* (Nazarite). These tractates are not exclusively about women, but they do contain laws involving women. Nedarim 10-11 includes women's rights to make vows and the process of revoking that woman's vows by husbands or fathers. Nazir is about women's ability to make a Nazarite vow and the stringencies involved with it. In tractate Sotah (a woman accused of adultery) are the laws for *Birchat Cohanim* (the Priestly Benediction) and *hak'hel* [9],

9. In antiquity, every seven years the people would gather together in Jerusalem to hear the Torah read by the king.

the public gathering for the reading of the Torah. The ceremony to determine if a woman is an adulteress is held in the Temple precincts, and so are the Priestly Benediction and hak'hel done on Temple grounds.

In the sixth Seder *Taharot* (purity) is the tractate *Niddah* (menstruant). At first glance one may think, "Why is this not in the *Nashim* Seder? This is all about women." However, the laws governing *niddah* are focused on ritual purity issues that happen to involve women.

Sederim

First Seder is *Zera'im* Seeds

Zera'im deals with agricultural matters. HaShem's holy people are tenants and stewards of HaShem's holy Land. They are expected to care for the land in the way that He has commanded. There are laws about how to plant and harvest crops, i.e., not to plant a mixture of different seeds in one field and to round the corners of the field so the poor might glean there. When the crops have ripened, some of the produce must be set aside and designated as holy, and the rest will be for common use.

Zera'im instructs how to separate the first and second tithes. The first tithe belongs to the priests. It also explains the process of bringing the second tithe to Jerusalem. If the distance is too great or the produce too large, it could be redeemed for coin and carried to Jerusalem. There are laws about separating *challah* (dough), which was the priest's portion. It defines from what dough it is separated, how to separate it, and how much to separate.

The first three years after a tree has been planted, Torah prohibits one from using the fruit of that tree. Zera'im defines what trees this applies to. It provides the laws of the First Fruit offering, what fruits can be used for this offering, and the rituals of the Temple ceremony in regard to this offering.

As stated earlier, this seder opens with tractate Berachot (blessings/benedictions). By placing this as the first tractate in the first seder, the rabbis focus attention on the necessity to bless God first and foremost before engaging in anything else. He is the source of all that is. This tractate contains the laws regarding the recitation of the *Shema* and the *Amidah* (18 Benedictions) as well as the *Birchat HaMazon* (grace after meals), which is blessings for various kinds of food that note the difference between whether the food has been grown from the ground or upon a tree, blessings for fragrances, and for different occasions such as the purchase of new clothing or a new house, and for things that are seen, such as when one sees a beautiful sunset.

Second Seder is *Moed* Appointed Times, Festivals.

Just using the words "appointed times" evokes the sense of spatial sanctification: a set-apart time. When the Temple stood, it was the center of holiness in the land drawing Israel from homes and villages to go up to Jerusalem to celebrate the Feasts. All males were commanded to go up for the three Pilgrim Festivals, Pesach, Shavuot and Sukkot. Today, there is no Temple, but our homes enjoy the same sacred space when we keep the appointed times. We draw down the holiness of Shabbat when we enter into it and choose not to go our own way. HaShem has called the "meeting," and His people would be foolish not to show up and draw near.

This seder includes the laws that apply to Shabbat, the Festivals, and special occasions. It tells how far one is permitted to walk on Shabbat and what types of work are not permissible. For *Pesach* (Passover), the laws of *matzah* (unleavened bread) and *maror* (bitter herbs) are here as well as the prohibition of *chametz* (leavened products). Here one finds what constitutes a valid *sukkah* (booth) and how to handle the *lulav* (one of the four species, willow, myrtle, palm and and etrog [citron]) on the Festival of Sukkot. It instructs in the fasts and commandments that are unique to each festival. Included here is the giving of the half-shekel tax. Although it was not handled on a *moed*, it was collected at regular and appointed intervals. One tractate deals with the reading of the scroll of Esther and the laws of Purim. Included are the instructions on how to write scrolls such as Torah, Mezuzah, and Tefillin.

Third Seder is Nashim (Women).

This seder is concerned with most matters pertaining to women: their rights and expectations as virgins, betrothed, wives, and widows, and the responsibility of the men in their lives based on their status. The status of women taken captive or raped is also discussed. It describes the process by which a woman accused of adultery (*sotah*) by a jealous husband is determined to be guilty or not. The tractates *Nedarim* (Vows) and *Nazir* (Nazarite) are in this order. They are not exclusively about women, but within them are regulations pertaining to women in their respective categories.

The tractates found here deal with the laws connected to marriage and the resulting obligations. Within these tractates are found the laws of Levirate [10] marriage, as well as the ceremony (*halitzah*) releasing the widow from that marriage. Nashim outlines the laws of *ketubah* (marriage deed), which provide for a woman in the event of death or divorce; included are also the laws of divorce.

Fourth Seder is *Nezikin* (Damages)
Jewish Criminal and Civil law

10. A Levirate marriage is when a widow is married to her husband's brother for the purpose of raising up offspring for his dead brother.

This seder is concerned with all manner of civil and criminal law, corporal and capital punishment for crimes, and what the requirements are for rabbinical courts and judicial proceedings. At the end of the seder are tractates about idol worship and avoidance of it as well the ethics and wisdom literature of the sages.

Just as the priests have a specific way of handling their duties, the nation of Israel is called by HaShem as a kingdom of priests and a holy nation, so the regular folk are also held to higher standards in their personal lives and business dealings. If a man had an animal that did damage to another man's property or person, the owner of the animal was held responsible, and the restitution was based on the extent of damage. This also applied to a man injuring another man, or a woman who was injured and miscarried as a result. In all business transactions, the seller was obligated to use just weights and measures.

Some situations discussed are:

- What happens when a lost object is found?
- Can the finder keep it or is he obligated to look for the owner?
- What if two men find it simultaneously?
- How is ownership determined?
- What if the found object was not an article but papers (documents of evaluation, letter of alimony, loan or court documents)?
- To whom does the finder return them?
- Is a man obligated to loan money without interest to a man who is known to be foolhardy in business dealings?

In other tractates are the requirements for people who will be witnesses and give testimony in a court of law, even the admonition given to them by the rabbis before their testimony. There are types of oaths that are administered in court hearings, private oaths, and oaths the rabbis instituted. There is a standard of conduct for HaShem's people, and the rabbis have attempted to address every conceivable concern so that law, order, and peace may be maintained in the land.

Fifth Seder is *Kodoshim* (Holy Things).

This seder details the laws of animal sacrifice, ritual

slaughter, and meal offerings. Included are tractates dealing with the laws of the Firstborn both for animals and men.

The Babylonian Talmud [11] is the only place where Seder Kodoshim is found; at one time it existed in the Jerusalem Talmud [12], but it has since been lost. This was already considered a difficult topic to study during the Talmudic period (30 CE-500 CE). Think of how difficult it is now, so far removed from the Temple service.

In tractate *Middot* are the measurements of the Temple and descriptions of the various rooms and what they were used for. The priests kept watch in three places in the sanctuary, and the Levites kept watch in twenty-one places within the Temple. The man in charge of the Temple watch would go around every watch with his lighted torch before him, and any man found sleeping was beaten with a stick and could possibly have his clothing burned.

There are thirty-six transgressions whereby a person may experience spiritual excision; many of these are prohibited sexual relationships, but the compounding of anointing oil or incense just like that made in the Holy Temple or anointing one self with that oil was also included in those transgressions.

Animals or objects that have been consecrated or dedicated for Temple use could not be used for common purposes. This seder is devoted to the holiness of the Temple service from sacrifice to incense, which extends into the sanctity of relationships, behavior, and one's own body. These connections are in the tractates that contain the laws of ritual slaughter for ordinary consumption and the laws of the dedicated ritual objects, such as tzitzit and tefillin.

11. See definition under "Talmud"

Sixth Seder is *Taharot* (Purity).

12. See definition under "Talmud"

Purity is considered another difficult area of study even during the Talmudic period. This seder contains the laws of ritual purity and impurity. Discussed are the ways different vessels can become subject to ritual impurity. There are ten levels of holiness, the Holy of Holies in the Temple being the highest and ending with the land of Israel; of course, the Land of Israel is holier than all lands. It describes how corpses can render people, tents, and vessels unclean and the length of time they are considered that way.

Taharot explains the construction of a *mikvah* (ritual bath), its use, and what can render it unclean. The laws of hand washing are taught. The laws of *Niddah* (menstruating woman) are found here as well as uterine bleeding not connected with one's monthly flow, and women who have given birth. Tractate Niddah, although all about women, is more concerned with how those events render her ritually impure.

This seder speaks of the one who has a discharge, e.g., gonorrhea or seminal emissions, and how that ritual impurity can be transmitted by contact or movement (the infected individual moves from bed to chair, etc.). The rabbis understood contamination and were well ahead of their time medically. The rabbis considered no subject taboo for consideration and discussion as to how those things might affect the people under their care and the holiness of the nation.

QUESTIONS FOR REVIEW AND APPLICATION

1. What is the most advantageous way for an individual to study Torah? What advantages are there to this?

2. Why did the rabbis hesitate to write down the Oral Law?

What caused them to change their minds?

Under what interpretation of the Law did the rabbis operate?

3. What reasons did the Dead Sea Scroll people have for NOT hesitating to record their texts?

4. Who was Judah HaNasi, and why is he important?

5. What is contained in the document Mishnah?

How is the Mishnah a continuing benefit for those who study it?

The root שנה means _____.

How does שׁנה relate to the way the Mishnah is written and studied?

6. Define sederim.

How many sederim are found in the Mishnah?

Define tractates

How many tractates are found within those sederim?

7. Define Halakhah.

What tractate does not contain any Halakhah?

What does it contain?

8. Seder Zera'im is about _____.

9. Tractate *Berachot* is found in what seder?

What does *berachot* mean?

What reasons are tractate *berachot* placed there?

Give an example of what is found in *berachot*.

9. What does *Niddah* mean?

What seder is tractate *Niddah* found in?

Why is it placed there?

10. Seder *Moed* is about _____.

Explain how you and your home may enjoy spatial sanctification.

Why is that important?

11. Seder *Nezikin* is concerned with _____.

How do these tractates apply to the daily life of an individual?

What are some of the situations that this seder addresses?

12. The fifth Seder _____ is concerned with _____.
Today this seder is found only in the _____ Talmud.

13. The sixth Seder _____ is concerned with _____.
Tractate _____ is found here although upon first glance it
seems it should belong in   Seder Nashim.

Define mikvah.

Who would utilize a mikvah and for what reason?

3

TALMUD

The Babylonian exile resulted in two vibrant Jewish communities and two Talmudim; one would be in the land of Israel later called Palestine, and the Talmud that developed there is called the Jerusalem Talmud, also referred to as the Palestinian Talmud. The Talmud that developed from the Jews in Babylonia is called the Babylonian Talmud. Both of these Talmudim use the Mishnah as their core text.

Out of the two Talmudim, the Babylonian Talmud is the one most often studied and cited. Several reasons exist for this. One reason is that following the Bar Kokhba revolt in 135 C.E., the Jewish community in Palestine was in tatters, and the rabbis recorded the debates and discussions only as far as 370 CE, possibly to 400 C.E. Unfortunately, some tractates and the entire last seder, Taharot (Order of Purity), from the Jerusalem Talmud were lost through antiquity. The Jewish community in Babylonia was much more stable, and the rabbis recorded their debates and discussions until 500C.E.

Gemara

The rabbis' discussions, debates, and exegesis, the rabbinical commentary of the Mishnah, is called the

Gemara. Neither Talmud has a complete *Gemara,* although there is evidence that at least on certain tractates it once existed. The *Gemara,* the rabbinic commentary from the Jerusalem community, is called *Yerushalmi* and the *Gemara* from the Babylonian community is named *Bavli.* It can be confusing to hear all of these different words, and since the Talmud contains both the Mishnah and Gemara, all of these words, including Bavli, have been used interchangeably.

In the Gemara, the rabbis explain difficult words or phrases from the Mishnah; it was written with as few words as possible for memorization purposes, and those students and teachers at the time would have understood what was being talked about. They expounded on the various laws, provided examples to help with understanding and application of the law, and explained difficult or unique words and phrases. They also are responsible for extending the laws of Hanukkah.

The Gemara faithfully reflects what was discussed between the teachers and students and between teachers and teachers. It is not a collection of stiff and anemic reviews of the law, but a real life interchange of ideas. The teachers and students may digress from the topic studied and expound on completely different subjects, bringing into the discussion information relating to astronomy, history, medicine, folk-lore, botany, philosophy, personal stories of family life, and a broad range of other topics. These men were learned in many areas, and they brought their knowledge and life experience to the schoolroom for the edification of all present.

The learning and conversation that took place at these academies touched on all aspects of human existence, as the rabbis understood Torah to speak into every facet of life. These men didn't just study together, but they lived in the same communities. Any questions, pressures or concerns their community experienced would be discussed. Therefore, each Talmud reflects the challenges of their respective communities within the centuries. For example, in the Jerusalem Talmud is discussion about Christianity, whereas the Babylonian Talmud is more interested in Islam.

The rabbis whose views are recorded in the Mishnah are known as *Tannaim*, which is Aramaic for "Teachers." These rabbis lived between 10 CE-220 CE in Palestine. The rabbis cited in the Gemara are known as *Amoraim* (explainers or interpreters); these rabbis lived in Palestine and Babylonia from 220 CE- 500 CE. Because the Tannaim lived earlier than the Amoraim, and therefore closer to Moses and the giving of Torah at Mt. Sinai, their teachings are considered more authoritative than the Amoraim. In the same way, the expanded teachings of the Amoraim are considered more authoritative than those delivered by modern rabbis.

Halakhah and Aggadah

The material in the Talmud can be divided into Halakhah and Aggadah. Halakhah is derived from the word, הלך (to walk), and represents the religious rulings.

Halakhah (how we walk) is Jewish law or religious law. These are laws that govern Jewish life, although it's really much broader. Although one can read a Halakhic ruling and know what he or she is supposed to do, permissible vs prohibited, many things are in practicality unenforceable. How do you make someone keep Shabbat or know if they are violating it secretly? How do you make someone eat kosher food or keep a kosher kitchen, or how do you know if they eat unkosher food when away from home? If one just views Halakah as what he must do, and worse as what he must do if someone is looking, then he misses the point of the commandments, which is to develop a person as a spiritual and moral being, bringing the light of HaShem to the world, thereby influencing everything around him in a positive way.

Aggadah is derived from the word גגד, which means to relate, tell and inform. The word haggadah (the re-telling of Passover in the service) from the Passover seder comes from this same root. Aggadah is difficult to adequately define, so most start to define it by saying what it is not. Any of the Talmudic discussions that do not fall under the category of Halakah (religious law) pertain to aggadah. Where halakhah is the practice of Judaism or the keeping of the Law, aggadah can be said to be the theory and ideals behind that practice.

The purpose of aggadic literature or discussions is investigation and then interpretation of the meaning behind practice. Included in aggadah can be words of encouragement, anecdotes of Talmudic sages, legends of Biblical figures, admonitions, parables, and proverbs, just about anything to encourage faith and bring about ethical conduct. Always the lessons are to teach the ways of our God and King.

QUESTIONS FOR REVIEW AND APPLICATION

1. The Talmud most often studied and cited is _____.

Why is this?

The Talmud contains the _____ and the _____.

2. What is the Mishnah?

The rabbis whose views are recorded in the Mishnah are called _____.

What does that word mean?

When did these rabbis live?

3. What is the Gemara?

The rabbis cited in the Gemara are referred to as _____.

What does that word mean?

When did these rabbis live?

4. What is the purpose of Halakhah?

5. What is the purpose of Aggadic literature?

Structure of the Talmud

Now that the framework has been established, take a look at the following layout of a Talmud Page.

12 1 2 3 4 9

7

בבא מציעא פרק ראשון שנים אוחזין

שְׁנַיִם אוֹחֲזִין בְּטַלִּית

8

שנים **5**

שְׁנַיִם אוֹחֲזִין בְּטַלִּית זֶה אוֹמֵר אֲנִי מְצָאתִיהָ וְזֶה

13

וְחלוקין

6

10

11

63

1. The Page Number. This section tells whether it is the front side or the back side of the page. At the very top of the page on the left is the letter ב. This indicates the page number, which is 2.

Notice the letter ב beit. In the Babylonian Talmud, the opening page always starts with the letter ב (beit) and then goes on from there, ג (gimmel), ד (dalet), ה (hey). In the Jerusalem Talmud, the opening page starts with א (alef) and goes on from there.

The letter beit ב has a dot next to it ‎בּ‎. That . indicates that this is the front side of the *daf* (page). We call this *amud alef beit*, (the front side of page two). The back side of the page has two dots like this : next to the page letter.

2. The Name of the Tractate or Volume. בבא מציעא In this case, it is Bava Metzia, the Middle Gate. (See Appendix A for a complete list of tractates)

3. The Chapter number. The next two words are ראשון פרקwhich indicates the chapter; in this case, *Perek Rishon* (the first chapter).

4. Name of the Chapter (usually one of the opening words in the Mishnah). The letters שנים אוחזין, Two Holding, is the name of this chapter.

This sample page would be cited in the following way: בבא מציעא ב ע"א Bava Metzia, daf ב, amud א, or Bava Metzia 2a.

5. Beginning of the Mishnah. This is usually the first word or words of the Mishnah; the word(s) is very large and embellished all around.

6. Gemara. Just under the Mishnah starts the Gemara (which are the commentaries of that Mishnah portion). It is often designated by the letters גמ׳. This is an abbreviation of גְמָרָה

7. Rashi. A Talmud page will be in a book, not just a loose leaf on its own. See this page as part of that book, and this is the page on the left with the binding to the right. The commentary on the right is from Rashi (1040-1105),[13] which is the acronym of Rabbi Shlomo ben Isaac. The script is different here, and it is known as Rashi script. Rashi's work remains the foundational commentary on the Talmud.

8. Tosafot. The commentary that is always on the outside edge of the page is *Tosafot* (additions); again see this page as part of a book; the outside edge is where this commentary can be found. Note the Rashi script for this commentary. Rashi did not have any sons, but he did have three sons-in-law, grandsons, and great grandsons; all of these men participated in the tosafot commentary, which was compiled over two centuries. Men using Rashi's system of exegesis expounded on his work, creating a very extensive commentary. It is often regarded as the "Talmud on the Talmud." It should be noted that not all of them agreed with Rashi's viewpoints.

9. Masoret HaShas   מסורת הש"ס tells where one might find a similar idea being discussed in another area in the Talmud. Unlike a concordance, which is word-based, this is topic-based and functions somewhat like "Google." It is used as a cross-reference for parallel and identical texts. A corresponding footnote will be found in the Talmud text.

10. הגהות הב"ח Haggahot HaBach are generally proposed corrections or revisions in the Gemara text, Rashi's, or Tosafot commentaries. The written Oral Law through the years was subjected to governmental intervention, and censorship causing revisions and deletions, and even simple typos occurred as it was copied and printed. This provides the proposed corrections and occasionally an explanatory, but brief, comment.

11. גליון הש"ס Gilyon HaShas are the notes pertaining to the Gemara, and the commentaries of Rashi and

13. See Appendix B for information on Rashi.

Tosafot. The comments are varied and are more often questions, usually ending in, "needs further investigation" or "needs much further investigation." Sometimes it will reference a parallel text similar to Masoret HaShas. Occasionally, the comments will encompass problems and contradictions within a text.

12. עין משפט נר מצוה Ein Mishpat, Ner Mitzvah is where the concept being discussed in the Talmud is codified legally, either in the writing of Rashi or of Maimonides [14] (the first to codify just the law in his work *Mishnah Torah* which is 14 volumes), the Shulchan Aruch (set table) by Rabbi Yosef Karo, or Sefer Mitzvot Gadol by Rabbi Moshe of Coucy (thirteenth century). "What is the law?" Means that many times in the Talmud we are given the opinion of one rabbi and then the opinion of another, but the text ends without revealing just how that Law was put into actual practice. This tells us where to find the answer.

13. רבינו חננאל is a classic commentary by Rabbenu Chananel [15]. Unlike Rashi, who may quote a few words or a short passage before commenting, or even Tosafot who discuss a theme, here the writings of the Mishnah and Gemara are reworked, and inside that text is commentary in full sentence format. This commentary can be read independently, and the reader will get the general idea of what has been discussed.

14. Maimonides is an acronym for Moshe ben Maimon, born in 1135 CE in Spain. He was an influential Torah scholar and physician.

15. Lived in North Africa (990-1055). One of the earliest commentaries on the Talmud.

If a Talmud page has different commentaries, don't be alarmed; almost every page will contain a Rashi or Tosafot commentary. Some of the other commentaries might be different depending on when they were published (1500's or newer) and who is the publisher. Keep in mind that when a newer Talmud is published, the publishing house makes every effort to incorporate any new commentaries within them.

The Talmud is an extraordinarily rich document, seamlessly weaving together the threads of rabbinic thought, exegesis, discussion, and religious rulings. The preservation of the Oral Law has captured life in the Second Temple Period, and provided the basis for legal renderings on difficult dilemmas today. It is not a document that one can easily pick up and start to read, even for a Hebrew reader.

The Talmud is best studied in a teacher to student relationship model. Otherwise, the nuances in the text will be lost. As Rabbi Yehoshua Perachiah is recorded in Pirke Avot, "Get yourself a Teacher." If one sets aside time for Torah study, his life will be greatly enhanced. The rabbis' dedication and self-sacrifice in the face of death to preserve the Oral Law demands a profound honor and deep respect.

CONCLUSION

What are we to make of the history and the complex structure of the Talmud, the primary Jewish source of learning the Torah? After reading a simple reconstruction of Jewish history, a summary word comes to mind: preservation. The formation of the Jewish Oral Law and its eventual recording into the documentation finally compiled in the Talmud preserved a people in their faith. It created a normative practice in Jewish communities scattered around the world.

Another facet of preservation was preserving the historic Temple customs long after the destruction of the Second Temple. Although the Jewish people were dispersed, the preserving of the Temple's day-to-day functions is an incredible feat, offering students of the Second Temple a glimpse into what it may have been like to live in the First Century.

The preservation of life is perhaps the most important aspect of the Jewish sources. The transgression of the Torah was so serious, that in order to protect people from transgressing laws that required a severe punishment, such as stoning, the Oral Law created fences, or boundaries, around the actual Torah commandments. The rabbis did not want anyone to be stoned or suffer severe punishments, such as lashes or excision from one's community and family; therefore, they created the rabbinic boundaries that would keep the people farther away from that transgression so that it would be much harder to transgress even by accident.

Although others may see the boundaries as onerous, the heart of it was to preserve life, not stifle it. That is the hardest thing to transmit to non-Jews who did not grow up practicing Jewish traditions. Because the rabbis were responsible for people's lives, putting up the boundary was important, for the Torah instructs every family to put up a boundary on a rooftop (or other dangerous place) where someone might fall and harm themselves inadvertently. It is up to someone who is aware of the mortal danger to erect a safeguard, an act of mindful care exercised even today in civil laws concerning negligence.

If one were to drive through Lexington, Kentucky, today, he or she would see something interesting. The most valuable horses in the world, the Thoroughbreds, are separated from busy highways not by one fence, but two, and sometimes three! The fences are well-maintained at all times, for if the horses broke through one fence accidentally, then another fence remains to protect them from being hit by speeding semi trucks and cars. This is not to limit the horses' freedom to run, but by running inside the fences, their lives are protected from accidental death. In fact, if a motorist were to hit a horse, the accident could kill those in the vehicle as well. In the words of Frost, "Fences make good neighbors."

Whether one chooses to follow the Jewish law is a personal decision, yet anyone can appreciate the heart commitment of the rabbis who learned, taught, and codified the "how to" of the Torah's terse instructions. They have created perhaps the most incredible historical reference document ever written in their preservation of the Temple practices. As technology presents new challenges in implementing the Torah's instructions, Jewish law continues to address the issues of how best to preserve life. If the life of a horse is valuable, how much more the life of a human being?

APPENDIX A

REFERENCE GUIDE TO SEDERIM WITH THEIR TRACTATES

Seder One Zera'im (seeds) Agricultural Laws

Tractate *Berachot* (blessings) contains the laws concerning the *Shema*, ("Hear oh Israel, the Lord our God, the Lord is One": a declaration of faith and a pledge of allegiance to the God of Israel), *Birchat HaMazon* (Grace after meals), and the Amidah (18 benedictions). It also contains blessings for a variety of occasions like when traveling; or when you see something beautiful or unique such as a beautiful sunset or rivers and mountains, or you have purchased something new like clothing. When we prepare to eat fruit that has been grown on a tree we say, "Blessed are you, O Lord our God, Creator of the fruit of the tree;" if it is wine we say, "...Creator of (the) fruit of the vine," if bread we say, "...Who brings forth bread from the earth;" if it is greens we say, "...Creator of the fruit of the ground."

Tractate *Pe'ah* (Corner) contains the laws detailing the rounding of the corners of a field when harvesting so that the poor might glean from those areas. Sheaves that have been forgotten in the field are left for the poor. The poor are entitled to glean at least three times a day from the field so that they do not need to sit and wait until the harvesting of that field has ended for the day. Some owners let the poor glean after each harvested row. Grapes and things grown on the vine and nuts may be harvested and distributed to the poor, not left for them to pick and possibly fall from a smooth bark tree or damage the vines and grapes. The laws regarding the tithes for the poor and all laws of charity are found here.

Tractate *Demai* (doubtful, doubtfully tithed) addresses a situation when an individual acquires produce from an *am ha aretz* (person of the field who is considered not to be as strict in practice or as knowledgeable of the Law), and he is not sure if all of the required tithes have been given to the priests, Levites etc... In actual practice the buyer could be made to re-tithe all of the required tithes and suffer a financial loss; as a result, the rabbis were lenient and only required the first tithe to be paid if the tithe on the produce was dubious to begin with.

Tractate *Kilayim* (mixtures) contains all of the laws which prohibit the sowing of different kinds of seed in the same field, planting different kinds of trees and plants together, and grafting different species of plants; included is the prohibition regarding the mating of different animals. Animals that are used in harness together to pull a load or wagon must be the same; even an animal tied to the back of a wagon must not be led by different animals. Garments may not be made of linen and wool woven together. Priests serving in the Temple may wear either wool or linen, but not together.

Tractate *Shevi'it* (Seventh, the sabbatical year) details the laws of the Sabbatical Year, including the command to leave fields fallow and what fruits and vegetables may not be eaten during a Sabbatical year. As all loans are cancelled as a result of the Sabbatical year, people hesitated to loan money because the debt would not only go unpaid, but cancelled in its entirety with the Sabbatical year. Hillel instituted the *prosbul*, a declaration which was made before a court of law by a creditor and signed by witnesses, the substance of which is written thus: "whereby the court, on behalf of the creditor, may collect the money owed anytime I wish." This worked as a blessing to both parties. It allowed the poor to borrow money anytime they needed it and prevented the rich from losing their investment.

Tractate *Terumot* (Contributions) are the priests' portions of the harvest. This tractate contains the laws for terumah, who can separate it, and how it is to be separated. It explains what to do if *terumah* becomes mixed with produce that has not been set aside.

Tractate *Ma'aserot* (Tithes) contains the laws of tithes, especially the first tithe which belongs to the Levites. From what time each fruit can be subject to tithe will vary with each fruit; some have to do with ripeness and others when seeds become visible etc... It details who is obligated to give this tithe and what of the produce may be eaten before it is tithed.

Tractate *Ma'aser Sheni* (the second tithe) contains the laws of the second tithe, how to separate it, and how to bring it to Jerusalem. The second tithe was to be used for food, drink, and anointing oil, all for personal use. It was to be used when one goes up to Jerusalem. If the produce was too bulky or the trip too long to Jerusalem, the items could be exchanged for money, but the money had to be used for the items mentioned or a peace offering consumed in Jerusalem. It could not be used for any other sacrifice i.e., sin or trespass. This tractate also contains the laws for the fruits of the fourth year. Since those fruits were also to be consumed in Jerusalem and the laws are similar to the second tithe, it was included here.

Tractate *Challah* (Dough) contains the laws of separating *challah* (which is the priest's portion) from the dough. Loaves made from wheat, barley, oats, rye, and spelt are subject to the laws of challah, which is a dough offering; how to separate it and how much needs to be separated are explained.

Tractate *Orlah* (Uncircumcised, pertaining to fruit) includes the laws pertaining to fruit trees that have been planted. The first three years the fruit may not be gathered and eaten. This tractate designates what trees this applies to and trees that are exempt, including trees that sprouted alone or those planted by gentiles.

Tractate *Bikkurim* (First Fruits) are the first fruit offerings that are brought to the Temple. They are brought from the seven kinds of produce for which Israel is known: wheat, barley, figs, grapes, pomegranates, olives used for oil, and dates for honey. There are procedures to bring them to Jerusalem and recitations at the Temple ceremony upon bringing them.

Seder Two Mo'ed (Appointed Times)

Tractate *Shabbat* (Sabbath) contains the laws for Sabbath; detailed there are the thirty-nine types of work that are prohibited, other types of work that may be associated with those thirty-nine, and what types of punishment are accorded with specific violations (7.1, 7.2). Included are three things a man must say in his home as darkness is descending on *Erev* (evening) Shabbat. Have you tithed? Have you prepared the *Eruv*? Then kindle the lamp (for Shabbat) (2.7). To understand the use of *eruv* see the tractate below, Eruvin. Included here are details about what is acceptable with which to kindle the Sabbath lights (2.1) and under what circumstances it is permissible to extinguish Sabbath lights (2.5).

The tractate *Eruvin* (Mergings) details the boundaries within which one may carry things and the distance allowed to walk on Shabbat. *Eruv* really means mixture. Sabbath travel was limited to 2,000 cubits from the boundary of the town. But if enough food has been prepared for two meals, and it was placed in an accessible place on Erev Shabbat at the permissible 2,000 cubits from the town's boundary limit, then this place where the food was located could be considered the family's temporary abode and would allow them to travel an additional 2,000 cubits on Shabbat.

Often families would place their food in a courtyard or alleyway along with other families, thereby allowing them to travel between homes on Shabbat. Modern Israeli cuisine was actually birthed from this practice! Before electricity was available in Jerusalem, Jews from Europe, the Middle East, and North Africa shared community ovens that held Shabbat foods warm. When the children were sent to retrieve pots of cooked food for the Shabbat afternoon meal, they frequently mixed up the pots, so Middle Eastern Jews were treated to Eastern European dishes such as kugel, and European Jews tasted the spicy foods from North Africa. Tastes for these foods developed, and the incredible variety of modern Israeli cuisine was born.

Today an Orthodox community will place a wire connecting their buildings so that people may be free to carry and walk on Shabbat. This is especially helpful for pushing baby carriages and wheelchairs, and it allows all to enjoy Shabbat together.

Tractate *Pesachim* (Pascal lambs and Passover) includes all of the laws of Passover. It teaches the laws of matzah (unleavened bread), maror (bitter herbs) and the prohibition of chametz (leaven). For example, leaven was to be searched for at night (using a candle) preceding the 14th of Nisan; if it was not done at that time, it must be done the morning of the 14th and then burned. When the Temple stood, two loaves of an invalid thanksgiving offering were left lying on the roof of the Temple portico; while they were there, people could still continue to eat leaven. When one loaf was removed, the people did not eat any more leaven. When both were removed, the leaven in the people's possession was burned.

All of the detailed laws of the Passover offering are found here, as well as the laws for the second Passover [16]. At the end of the tractate is the service for Passover eve.

Tractate *Shelaklim* (Shekels) is in this seder; although

16. If an individual were ill or on a journey and could not be home for Passover on the 14th of Nisan, one could still celebrate Passover on the 14th of the following month.

the tax was not handled on a *moed*, it was collected at regular and fixed times. There were shekel chests for collection not only in the Temple, but also in the provinces. We learn how those shekels were used in the Temple and what was done if those shekels were lost or stolen or an individual failed to give one year.

Tractate *Yoma* ([[Day] specifically *Yom Kippur* Day of Atonement) contains instructions for the fast and prayers to be said as well as the order for the Yom Kippur service that took place in the Temple.

Tractate- *Sukkah* (Booth) teaches what constitutes a valid and an invalid sukkah. A lulav contains a palm frond holder in which one places an unopened palm branch, willow branches, and myrtle branches. Together they are grasped with an etrog (citron) at Sukkot to fulfill the commandment of "taking up the lulav." A citron must not be all green, no smaller than a nut, and no larger than can be held in a hand (some rabbis say two hands). Sukkot numbers the animals to be sacrificed for each day of the festival.

Tractate *Beitzah* (Egg) is so named as the first word of this tractate is egg. It was known earlier as *Yom Tov* (good day), which is what we call festival days; and some laws that are applicable for all festivals are found here.

Tractate *Rosh HaShanah* (New Year) specifies not one, but four new years and what they pertain to. The laws fix the date for Rosh Hashanah and the descriptions of what types of *shofarim* (ram's horn or horns of a kosher animal hollowed out to use as a horn blown for varying reasons) are valid to be used for the different occasions.

Tractate *Ta'anit* (Fast) discusses public fast days and days when fasts are called, such as in a severe drought. It regulates those fast days and the sequence of additional fasts if the prayers have not been answered.

The tractate *Megillah* (Scroll) contains all of the various commandments concerning the festival of Purim, including the reading of the scroll of Esther. Since this tractate is about scrolls, the laws regarding the reading of the Torah and Prophets and the laws of prayer are included. It instructs in the laws regarding the level of holiness for synagogues and Torah scrolls. The laws about writing the different types of scrolls are here, too: mezuzah, Torah, tefillin, and the scroll of Esther.

In tractate *Mo'ed Katan* (Minor Festivals) are instructions in the types of work that are permitted and forbidden on *Chol HaMoed* (the intermediate days) of Pesach and Sukkot. Included in this tractate are some laws concerning the Sabbatical Year and the laws of mourning. In antiquity this tractate was known as *Mashkin* (to irrigate or to water) since this tractate opens with the laws concerning irrigating a field on *Chol HaMoed*.

Tractate *Chagigah* (Festival Offerings) contains the special Festival offerings a pilgrim would bring to Jerusalem: burnt-offerings and thanksgiving offerings. Included are the laws regarding ritual purity and ritual impurity so the pilgrim would know whether he was in an acceptable clean state to bring the desired offerings.

Third Seder Nashim (Women)

Tractate *Yevamot* (Sisters-in-law) details the laws of Levirate marriage and *Chalitzah* (the ceremony releasing a childless widow from marrying her brother-in-law). Included are the laws about forbidden sexual relationships, forbidden marriages, and conversion. This includes the process and testimony that are needed to confirm a husband's death so that his widow may remarry; without this, she is an *agunah* (chained woman) and forbidden to remarry.

Tractate *Ketubot* (Marriage Deeds) spells out the financial and personal obligations between a husband

and wife. The wording of the ketubah is important because it provides financial remuneration for the wife in case of death or divorce. Also included are the laws regarding rape and seduction.

Tractate *Nedarim* (Vows) details what constitutes a vow versus an oath, and how binding that vow is (what kind of vow is it?). The sages declare four vows not binding: vows of exaggeration, vows of incitement, vows made in error, and vows broken under constraint. We are taught when the vow takes effect and how it may be nullified. For women, the vows can be done away with by her father or husband. Depending on the vow, it may be nullified for a man by a Chokham (wise man/scholar).

Tractate *Nazir* (Nazarite) contains the laws of a Nazir. It describes the ways in which a person may become a Nazir; included in this are his speech i.e. "I will abstain from cutting my hair or from grapeskins." All details of the laws of the Nazir are upon him. Women can take a Nazarite vow, too. It delineates which prohibitions are upon a Nazir and what offerings he must bring.

Tractate *Sotah* (Woman suspected of adultery) deals with the laws of how and when this process may be applied and what happens to the woman as a result of the outcome. Found here are the laws of *hak'hel,* which is the public reading of select passages from Deuteronomy by the king (or the leader of the generation if there is no king) every seven years at the Temple during the season of Sukkot. All of Israel was required to attend.

Tractate *Gittin* (Bills of Divorce) handles how the bill of divorcement is written and the use of a neutral agent to act as a messenger in the delivery of it. This is very important, for without it, a woman is considered an agunah (chained woman) and forbidden to remarry, although her previous husband may do so. The original intention of this was not to punish a woman, but the idea was that a woman was sanctified to a man for her life, and as a result, he would care for her in every way. When divorce occurs, the rabbis want to make sure there is provision for the ex-wife. This also allows the woman to enter into another relationship with a man and allows their union to be sanctified. By putting the actual writing of divorce in her hand, the ex-wife has proof that she is legally divorced and her ex-husband cannot later claim that her new marriage is adultery and deny her divorce settlement.

Tractate *Kiddushin* (Betrothals) includes the various ways a woman may be betrothed. The rabbis say a woman may become a wife in three ways and a free woman in two. She can become a wife through money, a writ, and sexual intercourse. She acquires freedom to be a free agent though divorce or death of her husband. Included in this tractate are the laws regarding male and female servants.

The Fourth Seder is Nezikin (Damages) (Jewish criminal and civil law).

This seder is concerned with all manner of civil and criminal law, as well as corporal and capital punishment for crimes. It details the requirements for rabbinical courts and judicial proceedings. At the end of the seder are tractates about idol worship and avoidance of it and the ethics and wisdom literature of the sages.

Bava Kama (the First Gate) deals mainly with civil law. It determines the types of damages that one person can inflict on another, whether he did the damage personally or it was done by an animal he owns or objects he owns, i.e., a beam or pots. For example, if a man carrying a beam in the street stops suddenly and behind him is an individual carrying a jar, and as a result of the sudden stop the jar is broken, the man carrying the beam is liable. Included are the laws of assessment to determine the amount of compensation owed for an injury, a loss of a tooth, or even death.

Bava Metzia (Middle Gate) concerns itself with the issues that one would come across in the course of doing business: lost articles, sales and rentals, loans (including the laws of interest), hiring workers and tenant farmers.

Bava Batra (the Last Gate) concerns itself with laws regarding joint ownership, property rights (including right of ways), selling land to make a grave, inheritance laws, and laws regarding legal documents.

Sanhedrin (Rabbinical Courts) spells out the laws of capital punishment and ways these sentences will be carried out, i.e. stoning, beheading, and strangulation. It describes how the courts are to be established and judicial procedure.

Makkot (Lashes) is really a continuation of tractate Sanhedrin. It contains detailed laws about witnesses and those who give false testimony, the provision for the manslayer who killed without premeditation to flee to a city of refuge as his punishment, who is subject to be flogged and why, and determining how many lashes the person should receive without being irreparably injured or killed.

Shevuot (Oaths) focuses on the various oaths that can be made and administered within the courtroom for testimony to settle monetary matters, private oaths people may make, and oaths the rabbis instituted.

Eduyyot (Testimonies) is a compilation of many testimonies by rabbis on a wide variety of subjects such as slaves, bridal chairs, clean and unclean. Recorded are very unusual listings of instances when the school of Shammai was lenient in a ruling and the school of Hillel was strict. Historically the school of Hillel was more lenient in its rulings than Shammai.

Avodah Zarah (Idolatry) focuses on the importance of avoiding idolatrous statues, symbols, holidays, and gentile holy places. There is discussion on why one is prohibited from purchasing certain foods or wine from gentiles, in particular things offered to idols; it describes limitations and prohibitions regarding contact with non-Jewish associates.

Avot (Fathers) is more familiarly known as Pirke Avot. It opens with the historical transmission of the Torah. It contains the sayings of the rabbis, particularly from the Tannaitic period, and includes discussions of ethical duties and moral conduct, not so much Halakhic issues. For example, "There are four traits among those who sit in the presence of the sages: the sponge, the funnel, the strainer, and the sifter. The sponge because he soaks up everything, the funnel because he takes in on one side and lets it out on the other, the strainer for he lets out the wine and collects the lees, and the sifter for he extracts the coarsely-ground flour and collects the finer flour" (5:18).

Horayot (Decisions/Rulings) is concerned with the rabbinical courts and the decisions handed down. Of particular interest is the examination of cases where the Beit Din, High Priest, or the King of Israel erred and what kind of special sacrifices needed to be brought as a result.

The fifth seder is *Kodoshim* (Holy Things).

Zevachim (Animal Sacrifices) is one of the larger tractates; it details the laws of animal sacrifice, how the animals should be slaughtered, and where (north side of altar etc...) It defines what blemish, defect, or occasion would cause an animal to be declared unfit for sacrifice or its blood unable to be applied (i.e. blood of an unblemished animal mixing with the blood of a blemished animal). This tractate was once called *Shechitat Kodashim* "The slaughter of sacrificial animals."

Menachot (Meal Offerings) details all of the various meal offerings that may be brought to the Temple. Included are discussions of what may render a meal offering invalid, such as including too much oil or frankincense. It teaches how important it is for the priests to have the proper intention when handling the meal offerings. Contained in it are the most detailed discussions of mezuzah scrolls, tefillin, and tzitzit (3.7; 4.1) found anywhere in the Talmud.

Chullin (Ordinary, Unhallowed) deals with the laws concerning slaughter of animals not for sacrifice but for regular consumption; it defines what would render a kosher animal unfit to be eaten, such as injuries or disease; the prohibition against consuming meat and dairy together; and the requirements of what must be given to the priests. At the end of the tractate is the requirement to let the mother bird go if taking her eggs or baby birds, (Deuteronomy 22:6-7). This tractate was once called *Shechitat Chullin* "The slaughter of animals not for the purpose of sacrifice."

Bekhorot (Firstborn) is about laws for firstborn animals and humans, and any blemishes and defects that would preclude the animal from being sacrificed such as cataracts; it also lists any blemishes, whether permanent or transient, that would prevent a man from serving in the Temple, and the laws about tithing animals.

Arachin (Valuation) deals with the vows of valuation, in particular a few verses found in Leviticus 27: 2-8. What should a person vow to HaShem? How much? The valuation is based on age, gender and what one can afford. Included are the laws of dedicating items to the Temple. The laws pertaining to the Jubilee year are here.

Terumah (Substitutions) contains the laws that instruct how to substitute one sacrifice for another and what would render those animals unfit to be used.

Keritot (Excisions) deals with the thirty-six transgressions that are committed willfully that subject the individual to the punishment of excision, which is to be spiritually cut off from HaShem. It includes what sacrifices must be brought if an individual has committed these sins unintentionally.

Me'ilah (Sacrilege) details the laws concerning the unlawful use of objects or property that had been consecrated (set aside with intention) for Temple use. It teaches under what circumstances sacrilege may have occurred.

Tamid (Daily, Daily Sacrifices) contains the laws of the Temple daily sacrifices and the Temple daily service. We learn the three places the priests keep watch in the Sanctuary and the details of how the ashes are taken up from the altar, etc...

Middot (Measurements) gives the plan of the Temple (particularly the Second Temple) with measurements for the rooms and what purpose they served. Again we are told the three areas of the Sanctuary the priests keep watch in, as well as the twenty-one areas the Levites keep watch. The man in charge of the Temple Mount would check every watch with lighted torches to see if any man was sleeping on his watch. If he was found sleeping, he would be beaten with a staff and could possibly have his clothing burned as well.

Kinnim (Bird's Nests, pair of birds use for sacrifice) contains the laws pertaining to pairs of birds that were used for sin and burnt offerings as well as purification ceremonies for those who were ritually unclean, such as a woman after childbirth.

The sixth Seder is *Taharot* (Purity).

Kelim (Vessels) discusses in great detail the various implements an individual might use and the ways they can be rendered ritually unclean; it includes vessels in various stages of manufacture.

Ohalot (Tents) details how a tent and articles in it become ritually impure if a corpse is found there. This tractate also contains many details about how corpses affect many other things: house, people, courtyards, etc.. It defines how long the individual is considered to be in a state of uncleanness.

Nega'im (Tzara'at, Leprosy) details the laws regarding leprosy or "plague" found in people, houses, and fabric, and how they can be purified.

Parah (Heifer) details the laws of the red heifer and what makes one heifer acceptable for use and another not (such as a white hair). It describes the procedure of burning the red heifer and the ceremony using its ashes to make one pure.

Teharot (Purifications) contains laws regarding the ritual impurity of people and things. These laws are from the Torah and are also from rabbinical regulations. The items in discussion are multiple and varied.

Mikvaot (Ritual Baths) teaches how to construct ritual baths and the different types of water and other things that would render a *mikveh* unfit for use. In general the laws of ritual immersion are included here.

Niddah (Menstruant) is the laws regarding the ritual impurity of a woman who has given birth, a woman who is menstruating, and women who experience uterine bleeding not connected with their monthly flow. This tractate is not in the seder *Nashim* (Women) because the flow of blood is more of a ritual impurity issue.

Makhshirin (Preparations) describes how foods can become ritually impure from coming into contact with certain kinds of liquids. For example, a sack of fruit placed on the side of a river could become impure by absorbing the water.

Zavim (People Suffering from Bodily Discharges) deals with the laws of ritual impurity from those who have flux (secretions) from gonorrhea and seminal emissions.

That impurity can be transferred through contact when the afflicted individual moves from chair to bed, etc...

Tevul Yom (Immersed During the Day) deals with people who remain ritually unclean until sunset even if they have been immersed in a *mikvah* (ritual bath). Included are many discussions of how if a person who is *tevul yom* handles an item such as a vegetable boiled in heave offering oil, can render the whole batch unfit.

Yadamin (Hands) details all the laws regarding the washing of the hands.

Uktzin (Stalks, Stems) addresses the status of food and whether it has become ritually impure by the stem or stalk attached to it (the inedible parts); included are discussions about partially rotted fruit, etc...

Masectot Ketanot (Minor Tractates)

There are fourteen tractates termed external tractates or minor tractates. Although deemed minor, some are rather lengthy. The subjects they cover may have references to Halakhic rulings or Torah laws, but Judah HaNasi did not include them in his orders of the Mishnah. In a standard published Talmud, these tractates are located in Seder Nezikim. There are no commentaries on them.

Avot of Rabbi Natan expounds on the ethical concepts found in Pirke Avot containing the ethical sayings of the great rabbis of the Mishnah.

Soferim (Scribes) is the one tractate devoted to the history of Sefer Torah (Book of Torah); it contains the laws governing making Torah scrolls, including the writing of Torah scrolls and the establishment of the accepted Masoretic text. Included are the laws regarding the public reading of the Torah and Haftorah.

Semachot (Happy Occasions) is the popular, although

euphemistic, name for tractate *Avel Rabbati* (The Great Mourning). It is called this out of the reluctance to refer to a tractate with such a negative connotation. It deals with the laws that pertain to individuals on their deathbeds, internment, eulogies, funerals, burials and mourning in general.

Kallah (Bride) contains laws of marriage and modesty in sexual matters.

Kallah Rabbati (Long Tractate on Brides) is called this since it begins with the laws of marriage and modesty; includes laws of personal behavior, in particular, a scholar.

Derek Eretz Rabbah (Long Tractate on Courtesy) deals with laws of good manners, forbidden marital relations, and proper behavior.

Derek Eretz Zuta (Short Tractate on Courtesy) discusses manners and behaviors appropriate to a scholar. *Perek HaShalom* (Chapter of Peace) is found at the end of this tractate, and it contains statements on the value of peace.

Gerim (Converts) deals with the laws concerning the conversion process and the proper treatment of the converts, those called the righteous proselyte, and the resident alien.

Kutim (Samaritans) were individuals who the rabbis viewed as a sect between Jews and Non-Jews. The laws contained here are rabbinical.

Avadim (Slaves) contains the laws that pertain to indentured servitude.

Sefer Torah (Torah Scroll) contains the laws of writing a Torah scroll, in particular, words that must be written in a special way.

Tefillin (Phylacteries) deals with the laws of the head

and arm tefillin and the scrolls they contain.

Tzitzit (Fringes) is the laws pertaining to the ritual fringes.

Mezuzah (Doorpost) has the laws for writing the parchment scroll that is contained in the boxes placed on doorposts. It describes the proper place and way they must be affixed.

.

APPENDIX B

RASHI AND MAIMONIDES

Rashi was born in Troyes, France, in 1040. He owned and worked several vineyards that provided for the monetary needs of family. Amazingly, at the age of 25 he opened his own yeshiva. He studied in the academies in France and Germany. Although his hometown did not suffer from the Crusades, many Jews in France and Germany were impoverished, injured, killed, or forcibly converted to Christianity. When the Jews who had converted to Christianity (to keep alive) desired to return to Judaism, it was Rashi who championed them, encouraging the community to receive them without bias.

Rashi elucidated terms and words clearly and succinctly, using the methods of *peshat* (literal and straightforward meaning of the word) and *derash* (from the word to seek, an in-depth exegesis); he explained difficult terminology and provided background information when it was needed. His methods of exegesis are still used today. He wrote his commentary in Hebrew, and when Hebrew did not have the word for what he meant to convey, he would use an appropriate foreign word. To this day his commentary is read first following the text under study.

Maimonides is an acronym for Moses ben Maimon. He was born in Spain in 1135. He and his family first fled to Morocco to avoid Muslim persecution, then on to Israel, and finally Egypt. He was a physician as well as a Torah Scholar. He was the first to codify Jewish Law in a book called Mishneh Torah. A Jew could read through this and find the answer on proper behavior without expending lots of time searching the Talmud. As a result, some traditionalists feared his book would replace Talmud study. *Mishneh Torah* became a standard guide for Jewish practice. Maimonides and Rashi are still the most widely studied Jewish scholars.

REFERENCES

Adler, C. (Ed.). (1906). *Jewish encyclopedia*. http://www. jewishencyclopedia.com.

Bergman, M. (1986). *Gateway to the Talmud*. NY: Mesorah Publications, Ltd.

Cohen, A. (1975). *Everyman's Talmud*. NY: Schocken Books.

Cohen, S. (2006). *From the Maccabees to the Mishnah 2nd Ed*. Louisville, KY: Westminster John Knox Press.

Danby, H. (1985). *The Mishnah*. NY: Oxford University Press.

Herford, R. (1962). *Ethics of the Talmud: sayings of the Fathers*. NY: Schocken Books.

Neusner, J. (1988). *The Mishnah: a new translation*. New Haven: Yale University Press.

Shanks, H. (Ed). (1999). *Ancient Israel from Abraham to the Roman destruction of the Temple*. NJ: Prentice Hall.

Steinsaltz, A. (2000). *A guide to Jewish prayer*. NY: Schocken Books.

____. (1989). *The Talmud: a reference guide*. NY: Random House NY.

____. (1976). *The Essential Talmud*. NJ: Jason Aaronson, Inc.

Unterman, I. (1971). *The Talmud: an analytical guide to its history and teachings*. NY: Bloch Publishing.

ABOUT
THE AUTHOR

Rabbi S. Creeger's formal education includes an associate degree in nursing from Prince George's Community College; a certificate in Messianic Studies, bachelor's and master's degrees from Messianic Bureau International Yeshiva (MBI); and a Bachelor of Jewish Studies from Baltimore Hebrew University. She was ordained as a Messianic minister in 2000 and then rabbi in 2002 through MBI. Rabbi Creeger served MBI as a teacher, in the office of vice president, and as a member of the advisory board.

Rabbi Creeger has been active in several fields of ministry, serving as counselor and prayer minister in various jails, detention centers, and prisons in the Balt-Wash metro area and to returning veterans from Iraq and Afghanistan in VA hospitals (including Walter Reed) and VFW sites. She has also served as hospital chaplain in Cecil County, Maryland. She and her husband Boaz founded Messianic congregation Beit HaTorah in 1997, and they now maintain a Messianic presence in India and Africa, providing for congregational leaders and the people under their care with educational and training materials and providing financial support for food, clothing, shelter, and medical expenses. These outreaches include orphan care, including the Hadassah Orphanage in India.

Rabbi Creeger may be contacted through her website: www.beithatorah.org